DETAILING TRAUMA

T0154716

SIGHTLINE BOOKS

The Iowa Series in Literary Nonfiction

Patricia Hampl & Carl H. Klaus, series editors

DETAILING
TRAUMA

A Poetic Anatomy

ARIANNE ZWARTJES

University of Iowa Press, Iowa City

University of Iowa Press, Iowa City 52242
Copyright © 2012 by Arianne Zwartjes
www.uiowapress.org
Printed in the United States of America
Design by Ashley Muehlbauer

No part of this book may be reproduced or used in
any form or by any means without permission in
writing from the publisher. All reasonable steps
have been taken to contact copyright holders of
material used in this book. The publisher would be
pleased to make suitable arrangements with any
whom it has not been possible to reach.

The University of Iowa Press is a member of Green
Press Initiative and is committed to preserving
natural resources.
Printed on acid-free paper

Library of Congress Cataloging-in-Publication Data
Zwartjes, Arianne.
Detailing trauma: a poetic anatomy / by Arianne Zwartjes.
p. cm.—(Sightline books: The Iowa series in literary nonfiction)
ISBN-13: 978-1-60938-128-8, ISBN-10: 1-60938-128-9 (pbk)
ISBN-13: 978-1-60938-143-1, ISBN-10: 1-60938-143-2 (ebook)
I. Title.
PS3626.W37D48 2012
811'.6—dc23 2012004397

for my grandfather, george mccutcheon,
1918–2008,

and for dave

Detailing trauma. Things that can go wrong.
So many sites on the body map.

ANATOMY

This hospital, like every other, is a hole in the universe through which holiness issues in blasts. It blows both ways, in and out of time. On wards above and below me, men and women are dying. Their hearts seize, give out, or clatter, their kidneys fail, their lungs harden or drown, their brains clog and jam and die for blood. . . . Off they go, these many great and beloved people, as death subtracts them one by one from the living. . . . These dead loved ones we mourn were only those brown lower branches a tree shades and kills as it grows; the tree itself is thriving. But what kind of tree are we growing here, that could be worth such waste and pain? For each of us loses all we love, everyone we love.

—ANNIE DILLARD, *For the Time Being*

Elegy allows the difficulties associated with suffering—grief and loss—to be represented without closure. Elegy is the complexity of what is actually left behind. . . . When, suddenly, instead of the world revolving around a person, a person becomes aware that the world is chaotic and impermanent. Anyone she knows or anything she owns can disappear: the world's surface shimmers like a thin wall of water.

—KRISTIN PREVALLET, *I, Afterlife: An Essay in Mourning Time*

DETAILING TRAUMA

If you breathe you might get the burned ends of language in your lungs or in your heart or in the billion capillaries, the cords that tie the spine to the thigh, to the cochlea where you keep your balance, the mechanics of the middle ear, the throat so sore, the singing sinus, or one of the other important cavities of the body.

—ANDER MONSON, *Other Electricities*

body *n., pl–ies* By *body* I mean a plane, an expanse of our breathing and vehicle of our attempts at living, attempts at being and making our way through the tangle of people and questions and fears that is this world.

THE ANATOMY OF
TRUST OR BREAKING

1. Heart

The pulse shudders the body at such infinitesimal levels that many of us ignore its existence. Walk around carrying fists in the center of our chests, the bottom tipped somewhat rightward, sitting more-or-less directly below the sternum, squeezing each moment a red viscous liquid from atria to ventricles: from right ventricle into pulmonary artery, the only artery carrying deoxygenated blood away from the heart, moving to the cavernous surface of the lungs that if unfolded and ironed flat would cover the entire surface of a tennis court. Then there are bronchioles treeing and twigging into alveoli, inevitably described as little grape-like clusters, whose surfaces are bedecked with capillary twine.

Entering our bloodstream at those capillaries, our gaseous savior oxygen streams back toward the heart in our only oxygenated vein, the pulmonary vein, now from left atrium to ventricle, and finally with a steady shudder, a squeeze of left ventricular muscle pushes it in a gush through the aorta and out into the body. And every moment we walk around unaware and indifferent that a tide is pulling in our limbs.

Over the course of our lives our heart rate will change. Infants are human hummingbirds, little chest-fists squeezing one-hundred-twenty or one-hundred-sixty times in a single minute, tiny vessels filling and perfusing these small warm bundles of skin. As they grow, their hearts eventually slow, but not until adolescence does the heart calm to its normal adult rate of sixty or one-hundred pulses each minute. And as we continue to age, we climb back toward our infancy; in aged bodies our hearts have sped again, quick birds fluttering eighty or one-hundred times with each rotation of the secondhand.

Why (alight) is this the organ we've chosen as repository of our feelings? Whatever I harbor, I harbor here, thump-thump.

✳ ✳ ✳

What is heart to us: this one small organ, glistening and crowned with arteries. Thorny tangle. (This little clump of muscle, chest-lodged and unrelenting.) When we speak of heart. *At the heart of things. You've won my heart. My heart goes out to you.* Such a tiny, four-chambered thing. Ventricle mouths opening and closing like hungry carp.

If what we are speaking of is grit. *Take heart. She's got heart.* What we mean is stubborn doggedness, spunk, fight, clinging will. Pulsing red fist, desire: ferociously determined.

✳ ✳ ✳

I think it's the persistence that captivates us. The way a heart will actually restart itself if stopped. Sinoatrial node flashing bright little codes, sparks of imperturbable hope, electrical impulses to beat and live and keep on.

The ability to keep generating fresh hope amidst the din. Amidst a landscape that overwhelms. Hospitals & ambulances. Car window shatter & crumpled metal. Breakups, divorces. Thinning skin and the gradual erosion of memory.

To keep on inexplicably and despite the pressing weight, the dread. Stubborn, refusing defeat: if I only had half the determination my heart has. Half the grit, little round bundle of feist and fearless.

(It is at our happiest we have the most to fear)

Lately rock climbing, that passion, has me spooked. Halfway up a craggy, crystalled face, I find my hands gripping too tight to some edge, some crimp of granite, at a standstill: unwilling to move upward, above my protection, to trust what comes next. To trust that my feet will hold. That my rope will hold, my gear, my heart. Unwilling to pull up. To stand. Unwilling to risk it.

But if we start closing off. First climbing. Then driving? Next biking. Oh heart. The motorcycles, certainly. And travel. And loving? As risky as the others. Even now I feel its edge.

Closing can't be the answer. As persistent (and limitless) as hope. Closing folds in. Builds on itself. More pressing and heavy than what it's designed to avoid. It has no stop.

But what impulse, what hope to (hold fast) this fear in check?

Living as an act of faith? Ventricles squeeze and open without regard.

II. Liver

It always amazes me to hear radio commentators talking about the need for our economy to start growing again, as though it can be always increasing. As though increasing can be a permanent state of being. And as though we somehow, as a nation, are entitled to that. To that upness.

And yet in our own personal lives we are all too aware that up is a transient state. That our hearts are precariously poised. And that somewhere above are crushing weights, *glacial erratics*, boulders tipped up on end and balanced.

* * *

And so as we go about our business of falling in love—drinking beer together, walking in the desert together, waking up with dogs and blankets piled heavily on our legs—an edge of my brain is always already worrying at it. Assessing the tradeoff, calculating risk and regrowth. Heart, steeling against its possible future absence.

* * *

But perhaps, after all, the heart is not the best example on which to base our paradigm for loving.

Had we grown up in Morocco, amongst the Berber people, our declarations of love, of poetic exaltation or emotional disarray, would come from the liver. Similarly, during Elizabethan times in Britain, it was thought that the liver produced our blood—and that romance was aroused by an increase in the volume of the body's blood. Thus liver, and not heart, was the organ associated with love.

In some ways this metaphor seems more apt, though somewhat less lyrical— for the liver possesses its own kind of miracle. The liver, when damaged, is capable of regeneration, able to regrow into a whole functioning organ from as little as one quarter of its former self.

This seems a crucial talent for a body part associated with the bracing risk, the frequent shatter and rupture of love. To be torn apart and finally rebuild so fully.

After all, in the end—despite all our worry—mostly we go about our business of falling in love. We are not stopped. Even with some fear, the momentum is too great.

But this idea of *falling*—this, too, began in Elizabethan times. As though we were falling ill. Psychologist Frank Tallis describes love as a mine: ready to explode as soon as the tripwires of desire and longing begin to tremble. Of our phrasing, he writes: the innocent cadence of *falling in love* conceals a number of alarming truths about love that the unconscious mind readily acknowledges (and which the conscious mind ignores at its peril).

We fall in love, according to him, like we fall over, seemingly by accident—not by design. And when we "fall in love" we are again occupying the landscape of ancient Greece, where *theia mania* can strike us down at the whim of a minor god.

And yet we continue to take this risk, over and over and over. So to be able to regenerate after each explosion—to rebuild cells and tissues, to fill the hollowed out rooms and blackened doorways of the self—perhaps this is the capacity we need most, of whichever organ we identify as the mainstay, the nucleus of our emotions of love.

Dave is the person I am in love with. He is severely allergic to bees, wasps, penicillin, amoxicillin, erythromycin, Cephalexin, sulfonamides, azithromycin, doxycycline, & the rest of the tetracycline antibiotics family. Together, those are most of the antibiotics in use by the modern medical world. He's gone into anaphylactic shock six times in his life.

When we met, both of us had already loved many other times. Many other people. We each had some notion of the damage that can ensue.

Soon after we met, he decided he wanted to learn to ride a motorcycle. I gave him some very basic lessons in a parking lot. Two days later he was blasting up and down rutted dirt roads on a two-stroke dirt bike that had a few mechanical issues. For one, its throttle was hard to maneuver—either you were going full tilt, or stalling. I could only control that bike by feathering the clutch in and out constantly to manage its speed. Dave hadn't learned the subtleties of the clutch yet, so he just rode it at full speed. Throttle wide open. Nothing held back, and seemingly unafraid of damage.

I find myself more hesitant when it comes to risk. Find constant the impulse to step back, to close just a little, to anchor one foot firmly on the ground.

✳ ✳ ✳

In liver transplants, a portion of a living donor's liver is removed and used to replace the entire liver of the recipient. For children, this takes only about twenty percent of an adult's liver. But for adults, the segment needed is much larger. Sometimes up to sixty percent of the donor's liver. This, it is easy to imagine, puts the donor at some amount of risk. There have been a number of cases of donor mortality.

Would you give up a part of your liver to save one you love? Even at the possible cost of your life. Faced otherwise with the definite loss of their life. Most of us would say yes, at least in the abstract. The theoretical.

What about on a figurative level? Are we willing to take the same risk, whether it is heart or liver we use to fill out the metaphor?

How much do we put on the line—how fully are we willing to go in? *Love*, this dicey wager.

*   *   *

The happiest in my life. Is it brazen to say such a thing? And yet— even nights he is away, as I move about the kitchen, feeding the dogs, listening to the news, sipping crimson from a thin-edged glass and feeling its warmth soften my arms, then watching as darkness erases the yard—there is a kind of *content* to it all. (Dare I acknowledge—Is it tempting the cosmic irony of the fates to even say—)

And what am I risking, what damage to heart, liver, self as a whole —or self as *whole*—by saying so? The first small stars begin to prick holes in the body of the sky.

III. Nerves

Heart, *beating bird, little flutterer, now swelling open, now bruis-ing*—or salty blood, *that surging tide, feeding us, nourishing*—we romanticize the heart and blood, but not the breath and not the nerves. Why? Is it the vividness of the red, the security of the pulse we feel swelling just below the skin, the passion of it, when its beats increase or slow?

And yet the twining nerves passing from the skull through the *foramen magnum* give us our life as surely as the heart's incessant squeezing. Thick cable of sparks and flashes, running within the chain mail of the spine. Each vertebra of our protective spine sits on the next, padded by the cushion of intervertebral disks.

There is the body of the vertebra, a solid round, providing structure to the spine. Coming off that round, a ring of bone, with wings. The two wings, on either side, are *transverse processes*. In between them, a center fin: the *spinous process*. Palpate your back. Those are the knobs you feel.

Note here a slippage in our language by which *process* refers to a thing and not an action.

Inside that ring of bone passes the bundle of nerves transmit-ting a universe of knowledge: hand-lettered cards between brain and body, spelling out each motion, each sensation. Leaving the spine one by one, nerves exit the spine and travel outward and downward. From the cervical spine exit crucial peripheral nerves controlling breath and heart: thus the grim mnemonic used by medics, *C4, breathe no more.* The forking rivers and streams called the *plexus* give or take away the limbs.

You are still asking why, when at my happiest, I insist on writing of death. Is it a way of reminding myself to tamp the happiness, keep it in check. Is it an insurance policy: when some loss actually occurs, I will be prepared; I'll have traveled this terrain before, though with less urgency. Says Rilke: *be in advance of all parting.*

* * *

Scrivened arrow with its ribcage exposed: *consolation is not guaranteed, and despair is a real possibility.* Try for a moment to pin down the real color of darkness. *As if bounded in salt—*

Are we ever prepared?

* * *

I think this is a way of remaining in my body. Remaining present. Quieting fear. I can name the sections and segments of the body and the ways they might break. I can even picture, though I try not to, these ruptures happening to me, or to someone I love, someone whose presence is a part of my happiness. How does this make it better? Is this about "better"?

* * *

The disappearances of fecundity or hope there are many ways to be awake *(for is not all philosophy the study of death,* Socrates asked). Have you ever eaten a fig fresh from the tree, still glowing from the sun. Bite into it, pliant and warm, sugarjuice on the tongue. The fine crunch of many small seeds.

* * *

If I refuse to look into the dark spaces—the nooks of fear, the niches cloaking shame—then I have to create paths further and further around them. Avoid any reminder they are there. No terrain is safe. No line of thought, no language. Any thing, at any moment, might force me too close—those sinking places, with eggshell-fortresses around.

I'd rather keep them close around me. Make a blanket, a nest of them. Some level of discomfort then becomes the norm. Keeps the air in them open, fresh though bracingly chill. If I shut them off they become dank, anaerobic cysts in the skin of my world, burrowing and swelling, some node of fester I have constantly to negotiate my distance from.

✳ ✳ ✳

Through lively and unsparing questioning of our own ideas and motives we begin to discover who we really are the busking of wind in the branches. Every night there are dreams, exacting or woeful: limning of frost on the winter grass. Michel de Montaigne wrote, It is uncertain where death looks for us let us expect her everywhere *the premeditation of death is a forethinking of liberty*. Experienced climbers have rappelled off the ends of their rope. A friend said of another friend: *When he died I realized how thin our thread. Why do anything I don't truly enjoy?* Small birds hop lightly in the garden, peck at the yellow-bodied heirlooms.

IV. Lungs

Nighttime at a table with an old friend and wine and we asked ourselves: what is different now?

The carina is where the trachea bifurcates into the bronchi, one to each lung, beginning an inverted tree, branching and branching again, bronchi into bronchioles into alveoli. Into just the same shape we can look backwards, the branching of moments and choices, each one shaping our answer to that question: what is different?

Youth is a dream where I go every night and wake with just this little jumping bunch of arteries in my hand.

The lungs have no muscle. The lungs by themselves cannot pull in air. They need the negative pressure created by the diaphragm contracting, pulling downward, creating space in the chest, pulling air in. Similarly, accessory muscles around the ribs lift the ribs up and out: more space. Though we may experience ourselves as solitary beings, we cannot function alone in this world. Jose Ortega y Gasset sees us in *radical solitude,* a deep well of incommunicability and loneliness. Certainly it is true that when our last breath comes, the world around us continues breathing. But isn't there solace there? It does not all stop. The same heedless, tumultuous love we've felt, others will continue feeling. The same widening, at spring & bloom. And in consolation—Robert Kastenbaum writes about the natural credibility involved when consolation comes from companionship: *living proof that one is not alone when fearing loss of relationship.* We are not the only ones to lose—ourselves or those we can't bear to let go.

We can spend some amount of time gasping for air (*though we may experience ourselves as solitary beings*) the lungs alone won't get us there (*we cannot function*). Turn open your hand.

What is different?

This is one: I choose to trust. Different from the rash, reckless blind trust of youth. This is trust with eyes open. Trust that has seen the ambulance calls, seen the skin split open. Knows the pulp we can become. In body or in mind.

But knows also the expansion: the diaphragm contracts and the chest expands. Lungs open wide. To come open-handed and willing, to let go of suspicion. To step into the late-morning sun, yellow tomatoes ripening on the vines, figs purpling in the heat.

I choose to trust without drama, to let it be. When you offer to love me, instead of asking how? How much? How long? I say *thank you* and take the plantings you offer.

A few leaves curl in the desert heat *come wreck & rearrange* but in a riot of red *mostly there is fruit.*

⁎ ⁎ ⁎

. . . it's never that easy, though is it. Or, it is, and it isn't. My adult self, composed, experienced, sane, says *trust*. Trust and let it be. My other self—what is that one? Some infant shattering of brittle rock. Says *behind the drywall, behind the plaster*—as if I feared the hollow. I do fear the hollow but it is nowhere except in. Plans, lists, maps & driving directions are all a foil. *As if there were some safe order.* Some way to keep the world logical and safe. Some way to keep love manageable and *safe*. Things fracture.

Everything can fracture, though that doesn't mean it will. Here is where trust comes in. Or perhaps not trust but a willingness to risk breaking. *A crimson overlay of wrong flowers.*

rupture *n., v.* To say *rupture* is to refer to the many ways in which body breaks. Layers of tissue confronting the world. Skin, tendon, bone: we pretend we are not fragile. When I was twenty I learned how to frame a house, remember my surprise at how little structure actually resides behind the drywall. Nothing solid. Think of the body as heavy, dense, unbreakable in order to get through your day.

Explanation—Kauffman tells us: Rather than the more philosophical and perhaps enigmatic concept "awareness of mortality," we might use the concept of "mortality attacks." This is a more robust term, closer to the immediate painful reality of death.

IF LANGUAGE FAILS
US, OR BODY

I. Adrenal Glands

When will this wick of fear burn off? I wonder. November, and 6 AM, and I was on a plane.

A plane bucking and weaving and bumping its way through cold and early air, the spine of the Rockies vibrating into view through the windows. The two propellers valiantly fought to keep us aloft, and the fumes of jet fuel filled the cabin.

✶ ✶ ✶

We humans are mercilessly subject to our own body chemicals. Just let the brain suggest to the body that it release certain compounds—testosterone, progesterone, dopamine, adrenaline—and we are prisoner to the results: lusty or furious, terrified or blissful.

The adrenal glands perch atop the kidneys like a head atop a curled fetus. Along with the thyroid gland, they have the greatest blood supply, per gram of tissue, of any organ in the body. Named for their proximity to the kidneys (*renes*), these glands bear primary responsibility for regulating our body's stress responses. At the core of the adrenal gland, the adrenal medulla creates and releases adrenaline, and its partner noradrenaline, directly into our bloodstream.

Our response? Hummingbird heart. Rapid breath, a pale or flushed countenance. Pupils widened to dark plums. More blood to muscles, less blood to the stomach. Dry eyes, cotton mouth? The lacrimal and salivary glands are inhibited. The world tunnels in: loss of peripheral vision, and a loss of hearing called *auditory exclusion*. Pee your pants from fright? Acute stress response can cause relaxation of the bladder, even relaxation of the colon. Jettison anything that might slow us down: this is fight or flight at its most potent.

Though nowadays, it often misfires: we suffer from so many stresses that physical arousal can't solve.

✳ ✳ ✳

I was trying desperately to meditate on my breath, and trying desperately *not* to think about the breakfast I'd imprudently eaten before embarking. Also, I was battling to keep out of my head every story I'd ever heard about planes hitting huge pockets of turbulent, variable-pressure air and dropping a thousand feet in a matter of seconds. The day before, on the phone Dave cooly reported falling several thousand feet in a helicopter that lost power while attempting a windy, challenging toe-in landing, and regained control only after they thought it was all over. Certainly if he could survive that, I told myself, a two-hour flight in a small twin turboprop into Wyoming wasn't going to kill me.

My adrenal glands had other ideas. In the forefront of my mind were the words I'd heard David Sedaris speak on NPR the evening before, reading from his new book *When You Are Engulfed in Flames*:

The young woman was lovely and flirtatious, and as she pressed herself against the gate I imagined her lying upon an autopsy table, her organs piled in a glistening heap beside her. I now looked at everyone this way, and it worried me that I'd never be able to stop. This was the consequence of seeing too much and understanding the horrible truth: No one is safe. The world is not manageable. The trick-or-treater may not be struck down on Halloween, but sooner or later he is going to get it, as am I, and everyone I have ever cared about.

The plane heaved and swerved along; my ribs seemed to have a life of their own, curling inward like irony vines, sending out tendrils around my lungs and stomach. I held onto my breath for all I was worth: in, out. In, out. As much as I could narrow my world down to that one action. Either I was breathing, or I was not. As long as I was alive, I would have breath. As soon as I was not alive, no breath. Neither one of those options was particularly horrible to me. What was terrifying was the space in between: the terror itself, the seize of the iron bands, the conscious transition time from one state into the other.

Studies have shown that today's humans are not very accurate at identifying risk—actual risk versus perceived risk. We think nuclear power a greater hazard than driving a car. Rock climbing more life-threatening than riding a bicycle. Flying laden with the danger of mechanical failure.

Most of us do know, however—at least intellectually—that statistically flying is much safer than driving.

While I can tell myself this over and over, flying does not lose its grip on me. Its adrenaline. Sitting in a plane, bumping along at cloud level, I cannot pretend the world is normal. Safe.

I am not in control. I have no say. There is nothing I can do, physically, except sit still and control my own breathing. There is nothing I can do to change the course of things. I am in a closed capsule hurtling along at 300 miles per hour, 22,000 feet off the ground, and a flock of geese could take us all down.

II. Veins

We name off risk factors as though they will keep us safe. Consider the *pulmonary embolism,* a medical concern you may never have heard of. Much less ever thought would affect you.

Pulmonary embolism usually begins in the leg, in veins deep in the tissue. Because of the low pressure in the extremities, veins have one-way valves to prevent backwash. Clots tend to form around these valves and then travel.

The tiny deep-vein clot—made of platelets, blood cells, and sometimes bits of marrow fat—is called a *thrombosis.* As a piece of it breaks off and goes on the move, cruising upward toward the body's core, its name changes to *embolus.*

This little embolus is drawn inexorably back toward the heart with the rest of the blood supply. It is pulled through first atrium then ventricle. The right ventricle spits it out and pushes it toward the lungs.

Here in the branching and forking of the lungs, things begin to narrow. Depending on the size of our embolus, eventually it will get stuck. It tumbles down through the pulmonary artery, into increasingly smaller arterioles, and then the netting of capillaries hugging the lungs' alveoli like a seine. Somewhere in here, it lodges. Behind it, things begin to back up. Fluid under pressure seeps through vessel walls, into tissue and even into the lung itself. Downstream, no fluid flows, and so no oxygen is carried. Tissues begin to scream for air.

The amount of damage done depends on how large our embolus is, how high in the branching of vessels it gets stuck. If it is large enough, it may cause immediate death. If smaller: sharp, sudden chest pain, a sensation of being robbed of air, of breath. Eventually, a cough, a froth of pink lace coming up from the affected lung.

Who is at risk for this tiny, traveling clot? You could be, if you take long flights or are bed bound with injury or illness. Spend an extended period of time sitting or lying still, and the blood tends to pool somewhat in the legs, making it easier for clots to form. Long-bone fractures of the leg, because of constriction from the cast, long periods lying in bed, and the possibility of bits of marrow fat escaped from the opened bone, put you at risk. Your long flight to Asia or Europe, where you cursed the narrowness of the seats and aisles, certainly put you at risk, though perhaps you were offered in-flight beverage services or exercise videos with the aim of keeping your blood thin and flowing happily. Who is at risk? Pregnant women, whose blood is more prone to clotting anyway, and particularly those women confined to bedrest for a time during pregnancy; mountaineers who are stuck in a tent waiting out a several-day storm, and who already face the thickened blood and dehydration wrought by altitude; people who smoke; and women who use birth control pills, especially if they have reached the age of 40.

We name off these factors as if they will keep us safe. Check, check, and check: I am not at risk. Cross that one off the list of hazards lurking around every corner, behind each door, in the oncoming face of each car on the road. My friend Sioux described occasionally sleeping on the beach during her two years living in Hawaii: everyone was aghast at the idea. *They all told me it wasn't safe, I wasn't safe there at night,* she recounted. *But you know, no one ever bothered me.*

We spend so much time being afraid in our lives, we forget to enjoy what's around us, she said.

I was raised and schooled in the finer points of fear, and though I rebelled time and time again, the teachings are etched beneath my skin like a strong Catholic upbringing; with me continuously, though I try to quiet them.

Fear is a highway robber *we have only this one go at things* affixing the blinders & hinges to corner us in. Senses dampened and distracted *the sky breaks open above us.* Eyes called away. Heart too busy racing to be opened.

Perhaps learning the body, the science of it, the mechanics, is akin to the psychological quest to hold the dark places open, look into them, deprive them of their power. If I understand the ways in which a body can fail, will the dark places lose their fearfulness? Or, if I understand all the ways bodies fail, the myriad of ways in which we are frail and given to mechanical meltdown, facing my own physical breakdown won't feel so lonely. So terrifyingly alone.

III. Burns

Human beings are remarkably fragile creatures. Our flesh, for example, so easily burned.

One of the biggest concerns with burn victims is infection. A second is dehydration. Without our Saran Wrap barrier of skin, we are wide open and flashing neon signs.

The textbook I received for my EMT training, the American Academy of Orthopedic Surgeons book *Emergency Care and Transportation of the Sick and Injured*, 9th Edition, notes: "It is easy to become overwhelmed by the sight, sounds, and smells of burn victims. As you prepare mentally for a burn patient, prepare yourself emotionally as well." It does not specify what this emotional preparation should consist of.

Two hundred people died in the spring of 2009 in a wildfire in Australia's Victoria province. Burned cars, found run into trees or rocks and full of charred skeletons, or found empty with doors wide open. Spouses and partners on the phone with those at home, those watching the flames approach then lick at their houses.

I was obsessed with this conflagration while it was burning. Glued to the news stories. People were trapped in these fires to an extent that doesn't usually happen. Caught unexpectedly in fast-spreading flame, couldn't get out in time. Out of their control.

The flesh of burn victims can become charred and hard. Blisters the size of fists. Sometimes filled with blood. And elsewhere on the body, skin like wet tissue, peeling off in sheets, like a mummy who couldn't keep itself whole.

The textbook also instructs, "If your patient greets you in your introduction with a hoarse voice or is reported to have been in an enclosed space with a fire or intense heat source, these should be indications of a significant mechanism of injury. Similarly, if the patient has singed facial hair, eyebrows, nasal hair, or mustache, your general impression might be that the patient has a potential airway and/or breathing problem." Depth of injury can be hidden, invisible. If we cannot speak. If language fails us, or body.

The Australian news media report it was 120 degrees in the fire area, with 50 to 80 kilometer winds. "I could hear the fire coming through the forest toward the house," one man reports. "It was just like a jet engine . . . it was terrifying." *The classic burn patterns that we're seeing are mostly in people who've been forced to run through flames or who've been exposed to extremely high radiant heat temperatures.* "We were engulfed in a fire storm. There was fire burning on the side of the house that we fought for hours, but finally the wind changed direction and the whole house was destroyed. We were rescued after 22 hours . . ." *Everything is destroyed, it's like there was an atomic explosion.* "We found the remains of a woman in her car, right in front of our house, our friend who also lived on the property, who was last seen heading back to be with us."

When everything you've known or cared for is singed. Or annihilated. If you yourself are burned. The burned ends of words or nerves, capillaries cauterized, sealed shut.

There are these numbers we keep track of. Number of houses burned, 700. People injured, burned, sent to the hospital, 500. The height of the flames, 100 feet. Land area burned, 1200 square miles. Total body surface area of one man burned, 50 percent.

As if to quantify is to control. To make knowable.

As if by reducing the world to numbers we will tame its chaos, its unpredictability, our fear. As if we'll avoid being burned.

duration *n.* We move, in the words of E. M. Forster, between two darknesses: those who might enlighten us, infant and corpse, offer no word. And in between? *Duration* means something different on any given day. Today it means my grandmother is still alive in her gaunt body. Though as Roy notes of a chronically ill woman who asked to be let go: her request was an affirmation that to be bearably alive requires more than being just a functioning brain. Or, in the opposite realm of my grandmother's case, being more than only a functioning body?

Explanation—I have none.

THIS SUTURING OF
WOUNDS OR WORDS

1. Skin

My friend Nina archives & restores old films. Their bodies accumulate everything from dust to mold to dirt, shrink and become brittle, crack or start to break apart. They're decaying from old age. The sprockets along the edges rip open.

They store the old films in what basically amount to caverns in a cliff wall. The temperature is kept at 36 degrees and 10 percent moisture. The archive is buying time. Trying to keep the film bodies from aging, from decaying any further, before they can be copied onto another body.

There are so many ways we try to buy time as well. Not caves at 36 degrees, but almost everything else you can imagine has been attempted at some point.

Serums made from placentas. Cell injections from the tissues of fetal animals. Elixirs, ointments, drugs, hormones, dietary supplements. Cryonics. Alchemy & the use of precious metals for eating utensils. Monkey gallbladders, bathing in beer, bathing

in special springs. Injecting human growth hormone, or injecting botulinum toxin, into the skin. Rubbing in honey, or balm,
or ejaculate, to keep the skin soft.

The prospect of brittleness is terrifying.

☆ ☆ ☆

The collagen *microfibril*—left-handed helices twisting into a right
coil, triple-helix filament—this protein crosslinks into the weaving that is our skin. In growth and repair, in development and
disease, our skin stays soft, elastic, supple because of collagen.
When the body is damaged, it lays down new collagen fibers and
makes a scar: pale, thin, vulnerable layer of skin.

As we gather years to us, some of the collagen in our bodies is
lost, and some becomes more rigid, decreasing function.

Collagen's life is cyclical like most other things in our bodies.
We produce it and break it down all our lives. At some point,
though—somewhere around 40 years in—the balance tips: more
breaking down, less producing. On top of that, collagen in the
skin can be damaged by outside factors, distorting its coherent,
orderly structure. The sun's ultraviolet rays, chlorinated water,
smoking, and other types of pollution all do their damage.

Nature takes us from conception through our years of procreative
possibility with robust vigor. After that, our body's role, in an
evolutionary sense, is done.

There are varying theories about aging. One holds that aging
events are random, cumulative, and microscopic. That there is a
slow accumulation of damage to cell membranes. That chemical
reactions eventually bind together those molecular structures that
work best when separate: proteins, nucleic acid, and collagen.

Another theory proposes that aging is simply genetically programmed into our cells: they have a set life span, a genetic timetable. When melanocytes, the cells that give our hair its melanin pigment, wear out during midlife, they are not replaced. Grey hairs ensue.

* * *

(The prospect of brittleness is terrifying)

This year, I watched my grandmother shrink. She's forgotten how to eat, almost how to swallow; so tiny now, somehow she's hanging on. Brittle. Barely in her bones. What tenacity keeps her there still, keeps ventricles moving, messages pulsing to nerves?

In the same year, I watched my grandfather pass, unexpectedly, still so much more vital in his body than she. His eyes had gotten wider, his skin thinner; in the photos I look at now his smile seems a conjured motion—muscles of the face remember how, but the mind has started its own distance from the plane the rest of us walk on.

He was a firm believer in reincarnation and metaphysical knowledge. I remember, from very young, his stories about his submarine experiences in World War II. About the men who came to him and knew they were about to die. In the retelling, he would say my name, and then pause: "Arianne . . . I can't tell you how many times I had one of the guys come to me before we went into battle, and say, 'George, I'm scared. I think this one's going to be it for me.' And they were always right . . . they were always the ones to go."

His voice plays in my head still. His younger voice, solid, just a little bit of gravel.

We pump tissues full of silicone, needles into lips to keep them plumped, as though they were pillows to be propped up. Even after bodies are deanimated, we push fluids through the veins, some reason trying to hold them plumped, inflated.

II. Laceration

In older age, as our skin thins and becomes more delicate, more easily wounded, we may sustain "wet tissue paper" tears as a result of fairly minor trauma. But even before the skin thins and brittles with time, it is such a vulnerable body layer: soft, pliable, thin. We wound like ripe fruit, bruised and leaking open.

Lacerations to the skin may be clean and linear if they are caused by a knife, glass shard, or other sharp object. They may be caused by slicing at an angle, separating an entire flap of skin like a peninsula. Crushing injuries, caused by a direct blow or impact, may cause a stellate laceration, irregular in its course. If deep enough, a laceration may reveal underlying tissues: fat, muscle, tendon or bone.

Deep wounds sometimes accompany underlying bone fracture; it's even possible for the broken bone to *cause* the laceration to the skin, sharp splintered ends jutting through what was intact.

But broken bone is not the only way we are shattered or sliced. Whole worlds can fracture in an instant, leaving us reeling with lacerated ribbons of flesh or self. Whole worlds can fracture without a word of warning.

✳ ✳ ✳

The most striking thing about fracture is the way it arrives. You can be going about the most mundane day you've ever experienced in your life. Nothing unusual. Nothing to give you pause. Indeed, it's like every single other time you've ever done this particular thing you are doing—walking home in the evening, biking to work on a sunny morning, stepping into the car. You are thinking about other things. You are smiling at something your students said this afternoon. Or you are feeling your legs as they push against the pedals and extend, feeling your bike soar as you coast downhill. And then, suddenly—

Like a dropped fruit splitting open.

A rough voice on the sidewalk behind you. Or the shrieking scrape of metal against metal. Or the unexpected thud of something heavy hitting the sidewalk.

Once I was biking home through a grocery's parking lot in New Mexico. A large pickup truck hit me from behind. What I remember was the disorientation: an inexplicable physical impact, the instantaneous rupture of *normal*, the sense of being violently jolted apart from everything that I thought I was doing.

Trauma is a shear in ordinary blacktop. A fissure in the everyday fabric.

Like flannel being ripped. The shredding of each fiber in a mostly straight line. The frayed edges that result. The way the cloth loses its flat plane, becomes irregularly stretched and taut, gaping and baggy.

✳   ✳   ✳

When you get there on the ambulance you can see it in their eyes. The shock of it. The rupture. Like everything they've ever known to be true just dissolved into nothing.

A snowy road in Wyoming with red rock upthrusts on all sides. And then the wind swirls and the road is gone and all you can see is white. You can feel you're still moving. Posts swell into sight and then disappear again, just missed in the slide. Are you moving forward? Sideways?

Riding home and the bicycle and the ambulance in the street. The man with his patella torn open and apart. The foot so shredded it's no longer a foot.

✳ ✳ ✳

My brother's girlfriend called him the times she cut herself. Long streaking slices in the arms. He the bandage. The clotting agent. There are many questions raised of QuikClot and other commercial clotting agents. One type has been known to stay in the bloodstream, forming clots long after the need has passed, traveling eventually to the brain and causing *cerebral embolism* and stroke. Another, in powder form, blew into the eyes of soldiers in desert winds, damaging their vision. All clotting powder must be removed from the wound before physicians can suture, a lengthy cleaning process. Blooming wound on this terrain of skin.

✳ ✳ ✳

Sometimes fracture is a clean slice. Sometimes it is ugly. Unbearable to look at.

Unlike a house there is something behind the drywall. When a hand is blown open there is so much tissue still hanging there. Bones and connective tissue, sponge of the flesh soaked in red. Looking nothing like a hand but in the space where a hand should be.

Sometimes you approach the scene and a man hangs upside down between the crumpled metal of two cars. Sometimes other rescuers are already walking past him, as though he were not hanging there, as though no body upside down and hanging had once contained a person, an individual.

37

Sometimes whole legs sliced open, like cut fruit, melons spilling out of their cask. In the calf is so much muscle and so much flesh. Skin rolled back like curtains to a theatre of what is beneath. The soft and furled shine, the deformity. Visit a meat counter and you'll see what lies beneath.

* * *

Fracture is a sudden rupture in the skin of the afternoon. A crack, a tear, a rending apart of what once was whole. A violence.

III. Debridement

And after. After we are wounded, after our world is shattered by loss, reassurance is hard to come by. The precipice is still a precipice from the other side. From the bottom.

We find ourselves a shaky, knitted-together place to stand. Are, perhaps, a little purified, like rising from flames, by the absoluteness of it: by having lost what was unbearable, unsurvivable to lose, and finding ourselves still breathing.

But that's all we are, at this moment. Still breathing but broken, and at the bottom of this very tall precipice, with no clue as to how to ascend. Back to the flat plains of the living.

Back, with at least one foot, into the land of pretending again: we are safe, those we love are safe, there is no precipice.

* * *

Though some nights I wake fearful, wishing this city had less heroin and fewer gunshots, the truth is that fracture is everywhere. *Our hearts are our whole bodies and our wounds are visible.* We are atoms in a fragmented universe. Seen this way, individuals begin to blur. *Journalists use the term compassion fatigue. What Ernest Becker called the denial of death is a kind of reality fatigue.* And yet. And yet.

* * *

Doctors may choose to surgically remove dead or damaged tissue to promote the healing of a laceration. This is known as debriding the wound, and is most often done to create clean wound edges and decrease scarring, or to remove infected and necrotic tissue.

*   *   *

What is it that happens as fracture occurs. If it doesn't entirely break us. Though sometimes it does. But. Sometimes the shattered vessel fills with light. Sometimes the fracture opens us. Sometimes we become not less but more alive. Like the discomfort of standing on a high ridge, soaked in slicing grey rain, scoured by wind. Bracing. Perhaps this scouring can shed what isn't needed, sloughing off the dead skin built up over years of living, in fear of breaking, our faces turned away. *Throughout my whole life,* wrote Pierre Teilhard de Chardin, *during every minute of it, the world has been gradually lighting up and blazing before my eyes until it has come to surround me, entirely lit up from within.* This is a man who has known fracture. We live *steeped in its burning layers.*

IV. Clotting Cascade

The human body has a vast, astonishing capacity to repair itself. To heal. Wounds to the soft tissues of our body, to the skin, heal through a number of complex, overlapping phases. The *clotting cascade*, in which a net of collagen fibers forms and is pulled tight to stop the bleeding. The *inflammatory phase*, to cleanse the wound of debris, bacteria, damaged tissue. The *proliferative phase*, in which all sorts of small miracles take place.

Fibroblast cells proliferate, and help create a rudimentary layer of new, living tissue in the wound. *Epithelialization* forms a barrier, the epithelial tongue, between the wound and the outside world. Epithelial cells actually migrate across the new layer of tissue, advancing in a sheet across the wound site and also rising from skin appendages such as hair follicles and sweat glands. They climb over each other in order to migrate. The next time you cut your finger, imagine these tiny cells, scrambling one over the other to help you heal. The more quickly this migration takes place, the less scarring will occur.

At the same time, *angiogenesis* creates whole new blood vessels to carry extra sustenance to the cells fighting to repair you. This concentration of new capillaries is why the tender young tissue in wounds appears so deeply pink.

Finally, the *maturation and remodeling phase*, which can last a year or longer. In this phase, unneeded blood vessels gradually disappear, and the scar becomes less pink. The early, disorganized network of collagen laid down is replaced by a rearranged, cross-linked section of tougher collagen; as the wound heals, it becomes stronger, up to 80 percent as strong as the previous, normal tissue.

✳ ✳ ✳

Definitions for the word "recover" include: to get back something previously lost. To bring the self back to a natural condition. To return to a suitable or correct state. To return to a previous state of health, prosperity or equanimity.

But healing from wounds actually changes us. We are a different cluster of cells, blood vessels, and tissue once remodeled.

✳ ✳ ✳

How we choose to respond to the fracture all around us can be transformative. What we make of our own wounding. Which narrative we choose to believe.

One of today's prevalent stories is that of no-narrative. That everything is simply fracture. But I believe a different narrative is also seeping into things. Starting to clot and thicken. We take these stories to make sense of things. We take them to give us meaning.

✳ ✳ ✳

We are generations in conflict with ourselves: want to believe in a clear narrative and at the same time find we can't. Or, we spent so much time not believing. And not without reason. As we get older I think we begin to want—and to be torn. We understand fracture too well. Understand the shiftiness of any story, how slippery it is, how fickle. We've seen the places it can lose its hold, its meaning. The places where it's hollow. The places it avoids saying what needs to be said. *Like making love to reweave the frayed lace intricacies of a lie.* We were skeptics from the beginning. Still, there's this certain ache coming into place for us. An ache for something to supplant the narrative we don't believe in? Some-

42

thing coherent instead of cynicism, instead of a kind of social and relational nihilism.

*   *   *

The possibility that philosophical inquiry might confirm our worst fears (do we turn away). This heritage of relinquished blooms.

You can only relate what you saw *a bold and almost incredible answer.*

*   *   *

We've seen the speed with which images bombard each other, overlap, replace. The speed with which cultural amnesia takes hold. We know that *self* is a slippery thing. That the *I* can be no one, anyone, everyone all at once. Nonetheless, I think we're slowly finding we want it still to *mean*—as we drag this anchor across the bottom, we want it to catch somewhere.

*   *   *

If I say things thaw *the tap of salt water* am I trying to be optimistic. Though today a thaw is a frightening thing. There is the question of how to (hold to) optimism within the present world narrative.

Stitched and torn, cut and spliced the surgeon's hand is never empty. If you watch you can see the huge floes of ice, like buildings, come crashing down.

*   *   *

In the one hand I balance a brown egg: each generation has thought its world was going to end. *Paul of Tarsus called his days "these late times." He lived in the first century.* In the other, a speckled blue: scientifically, it seems this time around we have reason to believe it actually might.

Where do we put that in the narrative? If we are thinking say of children. If we've regathered that much faith. It all splits back open again. *Sutures today are made of specialized thread that will eventually dissolve into nothing.*

consolation *n*. The bones of the hand are numerous, immensely complex and delicate. They overlay and wreathe each other, a nestled cluster of carpals: *lunate*, *triquetral*, and *pisiform*. And yet these little bones of the hands, so many of them, pale in comparison: the bones of the soul *are like tiny fishbones . . . they have a hundred cracks upon a hundred cracks upon a hundred cracks.*

To hold one's pain is to sketch an entire anatomy of these bones.

Explanation—Saying *an inpenetrable isolation* is naming despair: nothing to fill this void, a world without luster. A thousand shattered small bones. As Kauffman directs us, the final treatment is in consolation, "found in the empathy and care of another human being." And yet we keep returning to solitude, inevitable or enforced: is this some form of choice?

CICATRICE & SCLEROSIS:
ON HARDENING

I. Bone

In 1939, a boy was diagnosed with *fibrodysplasia ossificans progressiva*, a rare and progressive bone disease.

Bodies of people with this condition "repair" damage oddly. White blood cells, instead of attacking foreign invaders, tackle the body's muscle or connective tissue. They carry with them *bone morphogenetic proteins* which trigger the formation of bone. Any bruise, cut, or tear to connective tissue is remedied with ossification.

The boy's body slowly grew sheets of new bone. It sheathed his muscles and locked the vertebrae in his back. His body armored itself in invasive bone tissue, living and uncontrollable. It slowly fossilized.

Imagine the weight of a step, a movement, with all that bone to carry around. Bone turrets and breastplates, a coral reef of bone building upon itself beneath his skin.

We think of bone as dead and stony, but we are wrong. Bone is very much alive.

* * *

There are two types of bone in the human skeleton.

Cortical bone makes up nearly 80 percent of our skeletal selves. The task given this bone is strength: to stubbornly resist bending or torsion. *Cortical bone* is a bronze dip, a protective coat, an armoring around every bone in our bodies.

A crosscut of this bone reveals the intricacy of Teredo petrified wood, filled with rings and patterned. *Osteons* like tiny eyes in side-view.

The second type of bone in our bodies is *cancellous bone*. Less dense, and somewhat more elastic, this bone is a rigid sponge, a delicate latticework. It grows inside the armor: in all our short bones, and in the broad, knobby ends of longer bones. And in our body's axis: skull, spine, ribs.

To picture it, think of wood that has been gorgeously tunneled out by carpenter ants: an osseous trellis, an intricate, porous coral.

Inside our bones, in the spaces around the latticework, is the marrow, a body of thickening, gelled lava. Glowing foundry for our blood.

* * *

Our bones are more fluid than we've ever imagined. A tide of calcium and phosphate washes in and out each day, remodeling them along their outer or inner surface.

They adapt to the mechanical demands we place on them, the tug of increased muscle mass. They store and mobilize our calcium rapidly. They are the art studios, the forging houses for our red blood, and the white-blood cells so vital to our immunities.

Rather than the dried skeletal mass we so often picture, our bones surge and flow with blood. Not only a clothes hanger for skin and organs—they are vitally interconnected tissue, entwined with all the rest of our constant sparking and flashing, feeding and fermentation, mitosis and metabolizing. Our ever-dynamic, our synthesize and demolish, our flux.

*　*　*

Ten years ago in central Taiwan, the earth shuddered and heaved in restless spasms. Its trembling measured 7.6 on the Richter scale.

I awoke in Taipei in the middle of the night wondering why I felt drunk. Why the room seemed to be tilting and shaking. Gradually I woke more, enough to think of an earthquake. I grabbed my blanket around me and ran for the stairs, out of the building, into a misty-rain parking lot already full of people.

Over the next two weeks, the earth seemed to move almost constantly. Every hour, or more, there was more trembling, quivering, heaving. Unpredictable. Sometimes nearly as strong as the first.

It was the duration of the heave that left its mark: every sense of solidity dissolved. Shattered anchor, what was once fixed, firm, steady. Safe. One afternoon I filled a glass with water, set it on my desk, and kept it there: my own little gauge to the earth's movement. Were we shaking again? Or was it just another queasy flash of vertigo. My body lost its sense of balance. I lost trust in the ground beneath me.

The National Information Service for Earthquake Engineering reports that nine-thousand aftershocks followed that first September quake.

In Taipei, we were lucky; there were few severe consequences, only a few buildings split at the seams. Photos from the center of the island reveal far greater devastation: bridge girders thrown, and their spans grotesquely twisted. Shear cracks, fissures, and weak-story collapses. The earth shrugged itself restively, tossed off our structures, as though they were light as bread.

To think of our bone as alive—constantly eroding and rebuilding, microcracking and repairing, as responsive to the hormones in our body as any of our other organs—is similar to the mental shift required after an earthquake, beginning to think of the earth as fluid, shakable, not-solid.

And if the earth beneath us, this dust-skinned body we walk on, prostrate to, build houses and roads leaning into the contours of—if this is not solid, what in our world is?

*　*　*

If this is not solid, nothing is. The downpour only increases.

Airplanes and cars are not solid. Families. Schools. Hospitals. Levies. This is the truth we live with every day. And try desperately to ignore, elephant in the room that it is.

The body you lay down to sleep in each night can go wildly awry. Tissues can go haywire. Wiring can cross and burn.

Bones can acquire a monstrous fecundity. Can grow rapidly, out of control.

* * *

The boy who in 1939 was diagnosed with *fibrodysplasia ossificans progressiva* was named Harry Eastlack. He lived for several more decades.

In the end, his body was so encased by calcium it locked him in. His jaw froze, his back was rigid. The bone growth began to press in on his lungs and he developed pneumonia. He died six days short of his fortieth birthday.

II. Alveoli

In determining pathology—the nature and origin—of medical issues, doctors will at times use the term *idiopathic*, meaning of unknown cause. Word that means no word, verdict that washes the heart in fear.

Imagine your body calcifying, hardening, with no understandable reason. Imagine facing the incomprehension of no information, the desperation for an answer. The desperation to be able to at least explain, define, attempt to synthesize some sort of story. Some kind of cohesive narrative. Some reason. We live by story and dying without story seems the most terrifying of ends.

☆ ☆ ☆

Ischemia, aphasia, hyphema, edema. The words sound pretty but what they describe is not. Our terms are like flowers on the grave.

Take for a moment *idiopathic pulmonary fibrosis*, which affects around 130,000 Americans. The lung tissue of people with this condition begins to thicken, stiffen, and develop scarring, or fibrosis. This thickened, fibrotic tissue gradually loses its ability to pass oxygen into the bloodstream; the alveoli, those tiny clustered chambers of the lung, harden. Radiologists, looking at high resolution imagery of fibrotic lungs, refer to the "honeycombing" pattern that reflects damage of the alveoli.

We don't understand the origins or development of this condition. Current medical thinking is that this inflammation and scarring could come in response to microscopic injury. However, any time doctors can identify a clear causal relationship (to things like smoking, exposure to asbestos or silica, viral or bacterial lung infections), that patient's condition is no longer diagnosed as idiopathic. Catch-22. There is also some thinking that idiopathic pulmonary fibrosis may have a genetic and potentially hereditary component.

Auscultation. Adventitious breath sounds, sounds of an abnormal lung.

Doctors compare listening to the lungs of someone with pulmonary fibrosis to the sound of Velcro, an interior crackling. The person's fingertips may have widened, often called "clubbing," in response to the lack of oxygen in the blood. The patient suffers from chronic shortness of breath, a sensation of not being able to get enough air. This condition can develop over weeks, or over years. In some cases, a single or double lung transplant may significantly prolong the person's life.

* * *

Three years ago, my close friend Nishta's father went into the hospital with recently developed respiratory difficulties. Three weeks later he was dead. There is no narrative here to make sense of it. To make sense of her loss, to make sense of his death. No narrative by which to say, he did this and this and this, but you don't so you are safe.

Our quintessential denial: we are not safe. Everything outside this breath, now, is uncertain.

* * *

Fracture arrives on silent legs. It arrives out of nowhere.

Sometimes it's a face. Someone funny, witty, and tender who breaks your world open in a second. Breaks it so far open and apart you're not sure how to put it back. To regain (reclaim) solidity. To make everything that was there seem like enough again.

Sometimes fracture arrives forcefully. Sometimes a telephone. Sometimes it is quiet. Sometimes a conversation, a sunny morning. Sometimes fracture is slow, no word at all, sometimes it is in what is not said. In absence. And sometimes it is sirens and lights and cones and yellow tape.

But not mostly. Mostly it's not that dramatic. There is a doctor talking to you in a real room with a real tree outside and the words she is saying are real.

The words she is saying mean everything has changed.

III. Scar Tissue

The *Manual of Intensive Care Medicine*, 4th Edition, elaborates on do not resuscitate, or DNR, orders: *Despite strong agreement in ethical literature and judicial rulings that patient preferences on forgoing aggressive medical interventions should be respected, this study reveals that physicians are often reluctant to honor such requests.* The book states:

The decision of whether or not to resuscitate is based on assessment of present or future quality of life. That subjective choice belongs to the patient.

These decisions are well within the scope of common medical practice.

1) They should not be elevated to the role of moral dilemma.
2) They should not be perceived as a judicial problem.
3) Patients should not be subjected to aggressive attempts at resuscitation without a reasonable expectation of successful outcome.

☆ ☆ ☆

We are so reluctant to let go. Compel treatment, action, anything rather than simply allow someone to slip away. *Slipping away* is a loss of control, like bones going haywire, earth turning not-solid. Groundlessness. And we are forever grasping after solidity.

(*Withdraws* like that; such a deliberate, peaceful word)

To surrender fully, to let go. To yield. Sometimes opening the hand is the hardest action the body can perform: one finger at a time.

* * *

This is to certify that I, _____, am refusing
_____. I hereby acknowledge that I have been
informed of the risk involved and hereby release the emergency medical services provider(s), the physician consultant,
and the consulting hospital from all responsibility for any
ill effects which may result from this action.
Witness _____   Signed_____
Witness _____   Signed_____

On the withholding and withdrawal of medical interventions, the
manual notes, it is "psychologically easier not to start than to stop."

This can also be the case physically.

For example, a too-rapid withdrawal of artificial ventilation pro-
duces air hunger, gagging, gasping, and struggle in a patient.

* * *

What is this all about? The fear of loss, what else.

Isn't that what we always come back to. Everything else circles it
restlessly. Wolves around a fire. If you are lost or if I.

If I love you and you go away then what am I left with.

* * *

A study entitled "Preparing Families of Intensive Care Patients
for Withdrawal of Life Support" notes that lack of preparedness
for death is associated with emotions such as depression, anxiety,
and complicated grief.

The nurses conducting this study tested various messages to help educate families on what to expect after the withdrawal of life support. The messages included information about signs of impending death: changes in breathing, skin color and condition, altered cognition, and declining circulatory status.

The study reports: *one of the participants stated that the information provided helped prepare her for the jerking, twitching muscles, heaving breaths, and cold temperature her loved one experienced. Another stated that he was glad he was prepared for the worst-case scenarios and relieved that they did not occur. He went on to say that he could see how not being prepared for the worst would make the death very traumatic.*

One study participant chose *not* to be in the room when his loved one died, feeling that the signs of impending death explained in the education message would leave him with unpleasant memories of the beloved. The study notes: *although the messages were designed to prepare family members about what they would experience, having such information also allowed them to make a more informed choice about being present at the patient's bedside.*

☆ ☆ ☆

If I love you and you go away then what am I left with.

If I am flattened by your loss, if I become dust.

What I am really speaking of here is *safety*. The illusion of, the grasping idea. *What is the fear inside language? No accident of the body can make it stop burning.* We think this thing exists, we premise (promise) our worlds around it, use it as our foundation, platform for our house, our heart, our body.

Just before we break there is a pause.

* * *

Every EMT knows *scene safety* is top priority in the system of patient assessment. For example, confidentiality is of the utmost concern in good patient care, *except* when there is a safety issue. The book instructs, "There is a *duty to warn* if danger of significant harm to a third party. Gun shot wounds and suspected child abuse have mandatory reporting requirements."

* * *

This idea of safety. Both bodily and otherwise.

We want to believe in it. Invent guns, and then gun laws; ambulances, padlocks, helmets, marriage. Things to keep us safe. And then do our best to turn our eyes, fingers in our ears, from the world which keeps telling us we're still not safe.

Or we obsess over our own fear: watch just one night of the local news. *Build more walls.* The haste of it, the ashen triage.

* * *

The Encarta World English Dictionary lists as synonyms of "harden": strengthen, reinforce, become stable, become resistant or resolute, become solid. In its second definition of the verb it says, however, "to become more tough, callous, or unfeeling." Clearly we are conflicted about this idea of *toughening*.

Build more walls.

We harden like lungs, like bone spreading through our bodies, to rid ourselves of vulnerability. Such tenderness, the human flesh. Such tender tissue, what we carry around inside. We are as fragile as newly-dried clay. A whole world of shattering lies around us; we see it everywhere we look. We can feel the fracture lines on us already, as though they are etched in invisible ink. But this is what it is to be human. The thick barriers we build, the toughened layers of scar tissue, only keep us apart. In isolation. The more we guard ourselves the more we become unyielding, inflexible, brittle from fear. Terry Tempest Williams asks, what kind of impoverishment is this to withhold emotion, to restrain our passionate nature . . . just to appease our fears.

If the world is walled out what is left to us? *The sky reveals itself to be nothing.*

impoverishment *n*. This is how despair works: it burrows, hollows out, like water running through sandstone until the swirling caverns and canyons run for miles and more. Until we feel we are in lack. By *self*, I mean that which is us. That which becomes us or forms us or defines us, thinking things that we are, seeking to believe as we stumble on each our own path. But we are more than just our bodies and our minds. More than what our ego lists off as "self." Simone Weil writes: *To love . . . through and across the destruction of Troy and of Carthage, and with no consolation. Love is not consolation, it is light.* She writes, *we must preserve an interior void.*

Explanation—So Ortega y Gasset, writing to a friend: Just as you are not your liver, be it sound or diseased, neither are you your memory, be it good or bad, nor your will, be it strong or weak, nor your intelligence, be it acute or dull. The I which you are, found itself with these physical or psychical *things* when it found itself alive. You are the person who has to live *with* them, *by means of* them, and perhaps you spend your life protesting . . . as you protest against your bad stomach or of the cold climate of your country.

THE PATHOLOGY OF
LOSS & LONGING

I. Appendix

The appendix is a strange remnant. An afterthought, a survivor, a vestige. Or is it? New medical thinking suggests that perhaps the appendix has useful function after all: researchers at Duke University propose that the appendix serves as a haven for useful bacteria, when illness flushes those bacteria out of the rest of the intestinal tract. Other researchers argue that the appendix plays a role in hormone manufacture for fetuses, and in the immune system for adults.

Either way, decades of appendectomies have shown that living without an appendix is entirely possible. The *vermiform appendix* is indeed worm-shaped; lives in the lower right abdomen; attaches to the large intestine; and is given to inflammation and infection. If that infection progresses, the appendix can rupture, leading to peritoneal inflammation, and then to shock, which, if untreated, can be fatal.

* * *

[A word on shock. It is common to say *I went into shock* or *he was in shock* about a wide array of social and physical situations. Medically speaking, *shock* occurs in the body when there is inadequate circulation of oxygenated blood to the tissues of the body.

This may occur with low blood volume, due to dehydration or excessive bleeding. It may occur with cardiac issues, when the heart is not up to its task of pumping oxygenated blood around the body. Or it may occur because of problems with the body's blood vessels—massive dilation resulting from severe infection, head injury, or life-threatening allergic reaction. But *shock* is always a problem of the body's pump, pipes, or fluid; it is not an emotional state, nor is it inevitable with every trauma.]

Fluid weeping into the body cavity: what happens to the system when something is lost?

* * *

One in fifteen people in the U.S. will suffer appendicitis at some point in their lives, most commonly between the ages of ten and thirty. Usually, their appendix will be immediately surgically removed in a procedure known as an emergency appendectomy.

And therein lies the question. Just what happens to us when we don't have an appendix? Seemingly, *nothing.* We live without it.

Does our body perceive its absence, do we experience any limit in ability, in immune capacity, in function? To the latter three, as far as anyone knows, the answer is no. We continue to function. Continue about our lives.

Does our body perceive its absence?

* * *

What does absence mean to the body—how does it keep count? Every day cells die and we pare them away. Osteoclast cells scrub our bones clean and then rebuild. We know that if a limb is removed, the body or the brain may experience phantom sensations, invisible pain. *Concerning the phenomenon of "forgetting,"* in some cases of phantom limb following amputation, subjects appear to be unaware that a limb is missing and, for example, try to walk on a missing leg. *The infant raises a shortened arm, and its mouth opens.*

What do we do with the nagging pain of absence? Where do we put it, how do we sit with it when it threatens to trample us underfoot. A sobbing restlessness under the skin.

* * *

And (if this world is *nothing more than a means of being in another*) how to remain present here after their loss. Dwell in them? Or in the space they left behind. Name pieces of our body for them: the notch in our clavicle, the hollow where they take away our appendix. Spaces where something is missing. I will call my ruptured vertebrae George.

(*Even when it seems there are no words that could possibly express the suffering associated with loss*) these words still beckon: blood, synthesis, grotesquery, despair, supine, beloved. Anatomy or melancholy.

* * *

What then do we do with language (*believing that holes can be filled with language is dangerous*) if not use it to fill what is empty (*only space itself occupies empty spaces*). To define what is empty.

Perhaps this is the danger: we seek to believe in language because it gives us the illusion of control.

* * *

Or perhaps it is the opposite. Perhaps to take refuge in language, to seek the rupture in language, is to keep this grief fresh. To remind ourselves that everything fractures—words, skin, the surface of the world. To keep ourselves on edge and away from apathy. Slicingly alive.

Move your finger slowly along the clavicle. There is no pulse here but to me this bone has always seemed one of the most delicate, its vulnerable protrusion from the chest wall, shadow in the hollow behind it, its tenderness should you press your fingers to it. You can almost feel the bruises forming.

The joints form bits of the body we typically take for granted. Start at the upper arm: its supporting bone, the humerus. There is no romanticizing of this space. We speak only of the muscle wrapping this bone in structure, its bulk, its body. Yet this bone makes possible the levering motion enabling us to lift the world to us. The head of the humerus sits into the *glenoid fossa*, forming the glenohumeral joint, a ball-and-socket arrangement with some of the greatest freedom of motion in our entire body.

The other bones of the shoulder girdle include the clavicle and the scapula. There are two more joints here: where clavicle meets sternum, intersecting at a tiny piece of terrain called the manubrium; and where clavicle meets *acromion process*, a tiny curve of bone curling off the top corner of the scapula. In addition, the scapula, only wings we as humans have been gifted, can rotate on the thorax, providing us some extra range for flight.

✢ ✢ ✢

Most joints allow motion, their articulation held together by the tough, thick tissue of their ligaments. At some joints, however, bones fuse together to form one solid, an immobile structure. Fontanels, as any parent of an infant knows, are soft spots in the head where the bones of the skull have not yet fused. A third type of joint is one with slight, limited motion; such a joint has bone ends held together by fibrous tissue, and is called a *symphysis*, of which the pubic joint is a notable example. In any intimate relationship the question is inevitably what sort of joint to become. Rotation is not possible because of the shape of the joint surfaces and the strong restraining ligaments on both sides of the joint. Although the amount of motion varies from joint to joint, all joints have a definite limit beyond which motion cannot occur. When a joint is forced beyond this limit, damage to some structure must occur.

Anne Carson writes: "as one moves into love, it gradually becomes impossible to identify with the other's innocence. From somewhere, almost inside it, stain soaks through. Who am I? His tears exasperate me. *You are good at being cold* he says and I say *Alas* and the famine is all around us."

✳ ✳ ✳

If you and I have not yet caused damage, in every past twinning there was some turning and twisting, restless rotation of each bone end independent of the other, neither long bone willing to settle into even, firm alignment with the other.

I've seen how the famine can take hold and I fear it. Fear my own capacity for winter.

But what does firm, even alignment mean? Does it mean the bones must be identical, settle together without interruption?

✳ ✳ ✳

Pathology is the study of the origins and physiology of disease, its causes, processes, development, and consequences. *Disease*, according to the dictionary, has its origins in Middle English. The term refers to a condition of an organ or system resulting from a cause such as infection, genetics, or environmental stress, and characterized by an identifiable group of signs or symptoms. An old meaning of the word, now obsolete, was "lack of ease," trouble. Dis-ease. A condition or tendency regarded as harmful.

A condition of an organ or system of an organism, characterized by an identifiable group of signs & symptoms. There are those who have argued that falling in and out of love could qualify. Lack of ease, that troubled state.

✳ ✳ ✳

Ortega y Gasset writes of the desperation and suffering of love but that is a different reality. That is love's burn. My struggle, and seemingly Carson's, is rather with love's stain. Or, the ice and distance in what was initially mistaken for love. Or continues to be called love.

What we continue to call love: jealousy, the desire for radiant attention; and simultaneously, a deep-seated, nameless shame; a turning from the light. And what this can all turn into: twisted distance. Cold. Disapproval. Shards of resentment, driving up through the skin. And more shame.

When a shoulder joint is dislocated to the posterior, there is often an associated fracture of the surrounding bone.

The question: can love last? is premised on another: can I, out of the depths of belief in my own stain—this fundamental unlovability—love? And all this fracture is premised on thirty years of audiencing: witness to a twinning with little generosity, less intimacy. I can at the very least see where my stories come from.

✳ ✳ ✳

But what does all of this have to do with body? With our softness, our vulnerability to tear, to rupture, to being pierced? Where is the meeting. Something to do with Carson again: the famine is all around us. But also it is in us.

Our fear surges when we recoil at the risk of physical rupture. But it is even more grippingly intertwined with our avoidance of the internal dark. The soaking stain of shame, the slicing fear of being utterly alone: unloved, unlovable. The rasp of what is torn, shards of glass all inside.

If we healed our inner rupture, would there be less need to pretend away the uncertainty in each minute? Or not—even whole, how can it ever be easy to face the possibility of impending loss? To love, and simultaneously, continuously prepare for love's departure.

* * *

Perhaps the challenge here is in choosing *not to prepare*. Despite the knowledge that departure could always, out of nowhere, come. To be present to what is, in this moment, love. To hold it openly, palms up. But to do this, do we have to feel grounded enough that we won't be annihilated by the loss? Or does *to live as human* mean being annihilated, over and over again? Like being born again and again—seeking some clarity, some fresh insight—skin shiny, thin, and pink after each new burn.

After each fracture we create anew our vision of *self*: like the falcon eye of Horus, swallowed by Osiris as Isis brought him back to life, making the first step of his new life the act of seeing himself. Nishta asks, "What is missing, the presence of which would make a difference?"

* * *

What is missing.

If what is within us is a fundamental sense of *lack*. If what we carry is a fear that, if seen, we would be unworthy. (A shadowy mathematics, to believe: in this *little nothingness*, some basis for desire.)

To say "love's stain" is just another way of saying: an emptiness. A closing off. A rupture.

(The one thing that keeps us out of connection is our fear that we're not worthy of connection.)

To minimize our losses we furl in. Tighten. But what else is there besides connection? What else does it mean to say *alive?*

This famine is self-created: we are starving ourselves out of fear. Whether to avoid the inner dark or the outer, what is being fled is vulnerability. The risk that in any minute of any day, we could lose everything. The whole of our heart or the whole of our body.

✶ ✶ ✶

They talked about the willingness to say "I love you" first. The willingness to do something where there are no guarantees. The willingness to breathe through waiting for the doctor to call back.

A researcher found that the one difference between those who live with a sense of relatedness, and those who struggle with connection, is just this: those who feel a strong sense of love and belonging, believe they are *worthy* of love and belonging. They feel they are *enough*. Imperfect, but enough.

They believed that what made them vulnerable, made them beautiful. They thought this was fundamental.

When we take the risk of opening. Of loving fully, wholehearted, even with the possibility of love's departure. Of allowing ourselves to be deeply seen. When we accept that there is always a struggle. That *perfect* is as much a myth as Sisyphus. *Errors of form, the pattern of a life.*

* * *

I think this is how the stain disappears, how the ice and distance begin to ease.

III. Brain

I recently heard a story on NPR. In it, a woman describes her last years with her husband. He had Parkinson's and also he liked to cross-dress. For her, these years were challenging and often painful.

At the end of the story, she stated: *As hard as life was, when people say to me, now that Doug's gone, you could date . . . I would never be interested in being with anybody else. Does that sound strange to you? It sounds strange to me.*

Doug was my . . . he was my beloved person. That's who he was for me.

Her *beloved person.*

I didn't ever think I would put faith in something like that. But now I find myself wanting to. Wanting to believe it. And wanting to profess—it's an act of faith, it's an attempt. We all know we're human. But sometimes we want to believe anyway.

* * *

What changes, in our brains and in our selves, when we find that kind of connection, a connection that is lasting?

Some researchers have speculated that we go through a sequence of love styles in our lives, from *mania* (obsession) in adolescence, to *eros* (romance) and then to companionship and pragmatic love in our middle years, and finally, later in life, to *agape* (all-giving love). But perhaps these stages are not limited to particular decades of our lives. Perhaps we're capable of circling around and around, as our lives and selves flux. Certainly, brain chemistry research has shown a significant obsessive component in the brains of people newly in love, be they teens or adults.

But what happens, what has to change, to make that love last? To make someone become a *beloved person*?

☆ ☆ ☆

A recent study out of Stony Brook University looked at the brain reactions of couples still in love after twenty-some years of marriage. The researchers began with the idea that long-term love and new love are similar, both stimulating parts of the brain related to reward and motivation. And they did find that, just like people newly in love, those in lasting romantic love showed activity in dopamine-rich parts of the brain—regions that respond to rewards, such as food, monetary gain, cocaine, and alcohol.

The researchers write, "these data suggest that the reward-value associated with a long-term partner may be sustained, similar to new love." They point to the definition of romantic love, *desire for union with another*, suggesting that sense of unity may become the "reward."

The researchers also found that, in contrast to newly in-love couples, these long-term lovers had *more*, rather than less, going on in their brains. They displayed attachment and "liking" toward their partner, in addition to the dopamine-rush of "wanting." They showed brain activity in an area thought to indicate emotions of warmth and tenderness.

Strikingly, the researchers also found activity in brain areas relating to self-awareness. This connects to a model of romantic love as rapid growth, the expansion that comes with incorporating another person into the idea of *self*. Such intense opening and enlarging is common early in the process of falling in love, as we begin to integrate the loved into our lives. It tends to decrease over time, however, as we become *known* to each other.

This research suggests that, in long-loving couples, the self-expansion can continue at a high level. That if both partners continue to grow, to see each other as new, and if the relationship becomes a part of their growth, the sense of opening and expansion can endure.

✳ ✳ ✳

Overall, this study indicates that longtime relationships can maintain *both* desire and friendship. That they involve *more* of the brain over time, growing in complexity instead of flattening. That couples still happily in love do sustain romance and sexual attraction—without the obsessive aspects such as "continuous and unwanted intrusive thinking" common early in romantic relationships.

Lastly, the researchers note that—unlike in new couples—they found serotonin activation in a part of these lovers' brains related to the body's response to pain and anxiety; that pain and stress reduction have been shown to be associated with an attachment figure; and that the set goal of the attachment system, as a whole, is proposed to be "felt security." Security in this world of turbulence and upheaval.

So romantic love, rather than being the hurricane, the up-and-down, the cause of *dis-ease* in our lives, can be our anchor. Some kind of solid ground.

✳ ✳ ✳

(Though, as we all know, even solid ground is suspect. Even the earth can shudder, heave, split into wide-gaping mouths, chasms and crevasses.)

But perhaps what that anchor can offer is a way to balance the fracture.

Because it seems what we return to, over and over, is learning to live with the insecurity. To somehow stay human, maintain a generous spirit; to somehow stay open, willing to be vulnerable, willing to love, even in the face of all this uncertainty. To find another way of being. What some would call *grace*.

* * *

We are not born. We are not annihilated. So where are we? Shards of glass on the edge of breaking. On the verge of refracting a way through, to another world.

Or another way of *being* in this one.

To believe this takes an immense act of trust.

* * *

To trust in our capacity to survive annihilation. To believe in this idea of a chosen other, a long-lasting love. Someone you take the risk of imbuing with so much value. So much weight. So much openness, connectedness, so much faith. And what then? They decide to leave, or they don't; they stay, they go away; this fractured, fracturing world takes them.

We are circling here. Circling what is central. What this always comes back to: the willingness to be broken open. Broken, over and over again, and to keep . . . what? To allow the tender pink skin to be seen. To not form callus over callus over callus, scar tissue thickened beyond any possibility of sensation. To keep allowing the longing to arise, instead of caging it, locking it away, suturing it into some tiny stitched thing we keep at the very core of us, cradled so hard it calcifies.

Because in trying to build *safety*, we give too much weight to our own anxiety. In believing there's some solid ground, if only we can find it . . . the quest is eternal, and doomed. Perhaps, after all, the only thing we really have is this choice, each time: to open, to love, or to not. To turn our faces away.

Talking around the fire one night with a friend whose second husband died of cancer, she said, "you know, there were many times right after he died when I thought about wishing . . . to have never met him. He was truly the love of my life . . . it was just so painful, impossibly painful, to think of life without him. But would I really choose to never have known him, give him up to avoid all that pain?"

The crack of landscape offers *storm & sunset, a bloody spill* (how do we bear this longing).

* * *

Try not to cover yourself in (famine or in) *breaking*.

attempt *n.*, *tr. v.*–tempted, -tempting, -tempts *Reality* and *perfection* are used by some as opposing terms. I object. Primarily to the very basis of the concept of perfection, which has led too many of us astray. We get one go at this. Why think it shouldn't be messy, complex, contradictory, and even grotesque?

A CARDIOVASCULAR
STUDY IN HOPE

I. Blood

Strawberries in a breakfast: the color of blood garnets, once used in arrows as indiscernible weaponry—hard to find & remove from the slippery of artery and its fluid. A tiny darted gem holding open its wound.

Sliva is Russian for plum, like a dark round purple hematoma, pupil to a bruise.

Like the coursing of oric veins, spidery gold on a red card. "My guru is within my heart, he is the viveka within my heart," wrote Jnaneshwari. "This means to me that our hearts are our whole bodies and our wounds are visible," says Fanny Howe.

*   *   *

Wounds are fed & cleansed by our supply of blood.

As are injuries. One of the problems with injuries to tendons and ligaments is that their blood supply is much less than other connective tissue. The healing process can be lengthy.

"Since all dying is a kind of murder by this world, I would like to be able to declare, 'I served another world,'" writes Howe later. So many descriptions of how tendons go awry (like rope over an edge, toothed up and snarled, or raspy sloe and swollen) & nerve tunnels. These elbows which just can't hold the strain.

Still blood courses through veins & arteries in circular, scrubbing and carrying.

☆ ☆ ☆

The ancient Greek word for blood was *haima*, hence our prefix haemo- or hemo-.

Hemophilia, hemoglobinuria, hemolysis. Things that go wrong with the blood. *We refuse to understand why living should be such a challenge to the muscles of the heart.*

But there is also hemostasis, stopping the bleeding, turning it from a fluid to a solid.

When a blood vessel ruptures or is cut, floating platelets in the blood come into contact with collagen in the layer of tissue around the vessel. They become sticky, begin to clump: a magnetism of bodies.

You may think of these platelets as heroes but they look like small monsters. Little floating horrors with many spiking limbs, a grotesquery of function.

Around the platelet clumps, a jumbled net of fibers form, like the tangle of northwestern forests. The platelets contract and pull the net tight. Our bleeding stops. The horrors have saved us.

Our bodies do much to preserve us.

Flannery O'Connor notes: *to recognize the grotesque you have to have some notion of what is not grotesque.*

Carson replies: *The grotesque may take many forms.*

Is it grotesque to think of our bodies split open at the seams, of what is inside now out? There is a certain grotesquery to the ways we break. But I would take body rupture over mind any day. *To speak of horrors.* The ways a diagnosis can spell a life.

Early-onset Alzheimer's begins before the age of 65. At earliest, its beginnings were identified in a 17-year-old. It is genetic, and runs in families. *No one outruns this disease,* says a news station. *No one survives it.*

To look at the world around you and know it is slowly being erased.

Your relationships to things, to place, to the language of knowing. That words and people will erode, go away. The *you* you think of as self, will go away. *The horrors.*

Yet with all these changes in the brain, the body keeps itself running. Though the appetite may be diminished, the patient still eats. Though perhaps fearful, the person still sleeps. Still walks around, perplexed, looking for something or someone they feel is missing.

And the blood. Irony red bodywater, surging and pulsing with vitality, carrying, cleansing, feeding. The blood itself keeps flowing as if nothing else has even changed. Grotesqueries.

II. Arteries

When my grandmother's own mother passed away, the blood in her arteries was so thick with cholesterol they couldn't embalm her. She was *always such a lady*, my grandmother used to say. Longing (soggy) dripping out of her voice.

Medically speaking, *the lumen* is the inside space of a tubular structure, like an artery. But look at its Latin meanings, its origins. An opening or a light: the luminousness of a space, the way light in the distance beckons, as when you have been exploring a cave for very many hours and approach the light of the exit. The air grows fresher.

The lumen of an artery expands and contracts easily as long as it is soft and unplaqued. All aflush, we haunt ourselves, seeking the distance between *knowing* and *unknowing*. Blood moves warmly through our vessels. Thin, sparse sliver of light.

As in our lives, the lumen of the artery sometimes becomes clogged with deposits, plaque, obstructed, obscured. We want to keep moving forward but sometimes it is difficult, almost impossible, to see the way.

* * *

(The city is nothing but a restless scaffolding) we forget where we are going. Lose where we are going. Cirrus smears the sky and blinds us. (How) do we ever know where we are going? You think and think and suddenly you are lost. On the radio today, a woman interviewing her husband who has Alzheimer's. Sudden heartbreaking lapses in casual conversation. *Oh, I told that one already? Today? Huh.*

The attempt at faith. *I know my children, my grandchildren will still be able to see the good person I am.* He was so positive I could have wept. I've seen where he is going.

✳   ✳   ✳

(Where to) is it only visible from the outside? *Forever opening* is one way of saying: hold open for, alight. *Keep walking forward* sometimes is the only answer. My mother spends several hours each day with her mother whose mind has gone. No. My mother spends hours each day with her mother who is only fractionally present. Still smiles. Still loves? Impossible to judge. But my mother loves her achingly *maybe I need her more than she needs me.* The world is leaking at the edges. *She loves me more than anyone ever can, or will.* Is this what mothers are for? Tender. To watch her wash her own mother's face is to slowly split open.

How do we see where we are going? At the end of a long time we too become motherless. Is this the most alone in the world? How do we say we *understood* and the morningstar keeps passing the horizon. And yet every lifetime people bear this one bracing solitude.

Thin, sparse sliver of light.

III. Pulse

We feel pulses at our joints because that is where the arteries are forced out toward the surface and around.

(Tenuous attempts at *belief*) the heart beats, systole, in our body's center; ventricles contract, and a wave of blood flows through our rivers.

Breathing that vexes the shoreline—*soft & scarred, dovetailing the light*—petalled and quiet at daybreak. Do we live by heart (does it hold water) or are we cells alone.

*   *   *

To speak quietly of *having faith* is to wonder: are we speaking of action or its opposite? To rise from bed each morning requires a certain degree of faith, an act of choice.

My grandfather told me he was unafraid of dying. Felt certain there were other lives, more growth to come. When a year ago he died in his sleep, he was lying on his back, hands folded over his stomach. He spent ninety years walking around this surface. Helping other people. Praying in the morning as he moved around the house, opening curtains, touching pictures of family members who'd passed on, helping my grandmother dress. *A kind of meditation*, he said.

*   *   *

To say *hope* implies a belief that things will be different, somehow, eventually.

As if to plead *don't let me be lonely* though loneliness is where I've found most of what was important. Where something got broken, and other things grew around them. Those pieces, little fruits, a shifting and a capturing.

—whereas to say *faith* is to indicate a kind of equanimity, a calm acceptance. A belief that we are more than just our bodies and just our minds? Or another way of being: open, curious, light with gratitude.

Though these selves break & heal, regrow and age, the blood keeps moving: soft, susurrus pulse in the waters of our bodies. Until our tide is done. *A kind of meditation.*

* * *

What does faith require of us, then, besides a willingness to break open. *Just that* as if it were a small gesture of the hand or face.

* * *

Once I asked him what he thought was the difference between a boy and a man. *Dependence versus accountability,* he told me. To be a boy is to think someone is always going to come get you out of your scrapes. To be a man is to have respect, and have a sense of responsibility to the people around you, people you care about.

(We create our own sparc slivers of light—luminous in so much bewildering dark.)

When he was young his uncle would send him across the street to help the neighbors. *They worked all day in the mines,* he would say. *They're tired. Go give them a hand.*

* * *

Lit up all around us, so many tiny slivers.

IV. Systole

The term systole is used in geometry to describe what is indescribable: an inequality of distances. It is used in literature to describe entry into the imagined, the surreal. In our human hearts, it refers to an unstopping, continuous wonder: the *wringing* of the ventricles, sending blood to lung and body.

The electricity behind the heart's systole comes from a sympathetic spark, an excitation running from the Bundle of His to the Purkinje trees (wondrous terrain, this body). Between the trees, the cardiac skeleton—a safety of collagen—keeps our wires from crossing. Protects our sparking life.

✳ ✳ ✳

We get this body and we get choices. As if we were a fraying of sun, some cataclysm of heat & motion, of light & pulse. Is the body a prison *errors at work* or does it let us free. Driftwood in a smearing tide.

✳ ✳ ✳

The heart beats, on average, 2.5 billion times in a human life. Each sparking, fluttering moment of systole, until we reach our count.

We get this body.

So often we avoid endings, as if that weight were too much to bear. *Do we believe in a beautiful world?* as if it were lovely enough to *die into. Lovely enough to balance the fracture.* As if there were something we might care about. A kind of *trust* which we would crush for exposing us, for holding us raw—waxed paper to a window's light.

✳ ✳ ✳

If we were to let go of the bloom. Skin as text and textile. Allow the autumn gusts *the accidental snow* the way things always seem to be *breaking.* Descartes wrote, *when the assemblage of the bodily organs disintegrates, the soul itself, in its entirety, withdraws from the body.*

Withdraws like that. Such a deliberate, peaceful word.

*   *   *

We get this body and we get choices. *Our lot.* Everything else, the subtle shift of pattern on bone, scrubbed daily anew.

(Though more things may be choices than we tend to concede) the longing of flightpath in this fissure of wind. *A kind of radical acceptance.* That every moment could be the only moment. That every moment could be the edge.

Blood courses freely through an open lumen.

We get this choice. To attempt, to risk, to be willing. *As if there were something we might care about.* A kind of hope we could carry forward.

Perhaps we can re-form the word *hope,* after all. To mean not a grasping for solidity, *a seeking after,* but rather a kind of willing-ness, again and again—sharp edges of beauty blaze everywhere amongst the shatter.

To remain tender, to cultivate joy *(luminous in all this dark).*

So many tiny slivers of light.

A form of meditation, this way of opening.

ACKNOWLEDGMENTS

To Aisha Sabatini Sloan, Leah Simmons Davis, Nishta Mehra: I love you immensely. Thank you for keeping me open/balancing the fracture.

A very large thanks to Boyer Rickel and Ander Monson. JC Olson, Betsy Thorlensen, Becca Iosca. Sarah Donnelly, Beth Alvarado, Barbara Cully, and Daisy Pitkin. Nina Rao, Sioux Adamson Towner, Adrienne Segall, and Beth Braun.

To Dr. William Zwartjes, MD, FACEP for his medical proofreading of the manuscript, and to Kathy Florance, RN, for the books. To the Wilderness Medicine Institute (and all its wonderful, immensely skilled staff) for the experience & knowledge I've gained while teaching courses with you.

To my family, for always holding up a mirror to me, and for being a source of so much of my continual learning & growth. With immeasurable love.

And, of course, to Dave.

Additionally, my gratitude to *Gulf Coast* and John D'Agata for selecting "This Suturing of Wounds or Words" as winner of the 2011 *Gulf Coast* Prize in Nonfiction; *Ninth Letter,* in which "The Anatomy of Trust or Breaking" appeared; *Terrain.org* for publishing both written and audio versions of "Clotting Cascade"; *Backroom Live,* in which sections formerly titled "Eyes," "Epithelialization," and "Maturation and Remodeling" first appeared; and *Umbrella Factory,* for publishing "A Cardiovascular Study in Hope."

NOTES

pp. 6–9 / Information about the liver comes from "Restoration of Liver Mass after Injury Requires Proliferative and Not Embryonic Transcriptional Patterns" by Hasan H. Otu, Kamila Naxerova, Karen Ho, Handan Can, Nicole Nesbitt, Towia A. Libermann, and Seth J. Karp.

pp. 6–7 / Dr. Frank Tallis, in his book *Love Sick: Love as a Mental Illness*, writes of Elizabethan beliefs about blood, romance, and the liver.

p. 7 / In *Love Sick*, Tallis also writes, "the innocent cadence of *falling in love* conceals a number of alarming truths about love which the unconscious mind readily acknowledges (and which the conscious mind ignores at its peril). We fall in love," according to him, "like we fall over, seemingly by accident—not by design. When we 'fall in love' we are again occupying the landscape of ancient Greece, where *theia mania* can strike us down at the whim of a minor god."

p. 13 / From the endeavor of philosophical inquiry, "consolation is not guaranteed, and despair is a real possibility," writes Robert Kastenbaum in *Awareness of Mortality*. He cites Plato's *Republic: For is not all philosophy the study of death, Socrates asked.* He also quotes Michel de Montaigne from the *First Book of the Essays of Michael, Lord of Montaigne*: "It is uncertaine where death looks for us; let us expect her everie where: the premeditation of death, is a fore-thinking of libertie."

p. 13 / *Youth is a dream where I go every night and wake with just this little jumping bunch of arteries in my hand* comes from Anne Carson's *Plainwater*.

p. 13 / In "Immortality," an essay in *Awareness of Mortality*, John Morgan writes, "Jose Ortega y Gassett described the person as a 'radical solitude,' that is, at the very root (radix) of us, there is an ultimate incommunicability and loneliness."

p. 13 / "There is a 'natural credibility' involved . . ." comes from Kastenbaum's essay "What Should We Expect from Philosophy?" in *Awareness of Mortality*.

p. 14 / *Plans, lists, maps and driving directions* is a phrase borrowed from Jenny Boully's *The Book of Beginnings and Endings*.

p. 17 / In Jeffrey Kauffman's opening to Part I of *Awareness of Mortality*, which he edited, he introduces Kastenbaum's concept of "mortality attacks."

p. 19 / *When will this wick of fear burn off?, I wonder* is from *Remanence* by Boyer Rickel.

pp. 19–20 / Adrenal facts are from the book *Surgical Anatomy and Technique* by L. J. Skandalakis, L. E. Skandalakis, and P. N. Skandalakis.

p. 21 / "Studies have shown . . ." refers to Paul Slovic's article "Perception of Risk," which appeared in *Science Magazine* in 1987.

p. 27 / Quotes and statistics come from the following BBC news stories: "Slideshow: Fleeing the Flames," "Eyewitness Stories: Australia Fires," and "Bushfire Dilemma: Flee or Fight." These articles appeared in February of 2009.

p. 29 / The passage that begins, "We move between two darknesses . . ." is a very slight paraphrase of E. M. Forster, as he is quoted on page 39 of Annie Dillard's *For the Time Being*.

p. 29 / David Roy's reflections on a chronically ill patient come from "Dying and Death—Late in the Twentieth Century," in *Awareness of Mortality*.

p. 32 / Information on the collagen microfibril comes from *Structure, Stability and Folding of the Collagen Triple Helix*, by Jürgen Engel and Hans Peter Bächinger.

pp. 32–33 / Information on theories of aging comes from *Human Growth and Development through the Lifespan*, by Kathleen Thies and John Travers.

p. 39 / *Journalists use the term compassion fatigue. What Ernest Becker called the denial of death is a kind of reality fatigue* is from Dillard's *For the Time Being*.

p. 40 / In *For the Time Being*, Dillard quotes Teilhard de Chardin as writing of the divine: *Throughout my whole life, during every minute of it, the world has been gradually lighting up and blazing before my eyes until it has come to surround me, entirely lit up from within.* He continues: *We imagined it as distant and inaccessible, whereas in fact we live steeped in its burning layers.*

p. 42 / *Like making love to reweave the frayed lace intricacies of a lie* comes from Rickel's book *Remanence*.

p. 43 / *Paul of Tarsus called his days "these late times." He lived in the first century* is from Dillard's *For the Time Being*.

p. 45 / *And yet these little bones of the hands, so many of them, pale in comparison: the bones of the soul are like tiny fishbones . . . they have a hundred cracks upon a hundred cracks upon a hundred cracks*, is an adaptation of the words of psychotherapist Adrienne Segall.

pp. 47, 51 / Much of the information on *fibrodysplasia ossificans progressiva* and Harry Eastlack comes from a March 1999 BBC article entitled "Shark Therapy for Bizarre Bone Disease." The April 2009 *New York Times* article that first brought this story to my attention was "Bone: A Masterpiece of Elastic Strength," by Natalie Angiers.

pp. 48–49 / Information on bone types comes from the website of MEDES, the Institute for Space Medicine and Physiology. Information on bone remodeling is from *Medical Physiology*, third edition, by Rodney Rhoades and David R. Bell.

pp. 52–53 / Information in "Alveoli" comes from Dr. Andrew Limper of the Pulmonary and Critical Care Medicine division of the Mayo Clinic; from the Pulmonary Fibrosis Foundation; and from the study "Lung Transplantation for Idiopathic Pulmonary Fibrosis" in *The Annals of Thoracic Surgery* by David P. Mason et al.

p. 56 / The study I cite here, "Preparing Families of Intensive Care Patients for Withdrawal of Life Support" by Karin T. Kirchhoff et al., comes from the March 1, 2008 issue of *American Journal of Critical Care*.

p. 57 / *What is the fear inside language? No accident of the body can make it stop burning* is from Carson's *Plainwater*.

p. 58 / "The book instructs . . ." is from the *Manual of Intensive Care Medicine*, fourth edition, by Richard S. Irwin and James M. Rippe.

p. 59 / The Terry Tempest Williams quote about impoverishment is from her book, *An Unspoken Hunger*.

p. 59 / *The sky reveals itself to be nothing* is taken from Boully's *The Book of Beginnings and Endings*.

p. 61 / This quote by Simone Weil comes from her book, *Gravity & Grace*. The Ortega y Gassett quote comes from *The Dehumanization of Art and Other Writings on Art and Culture*.

pp. 63–64 / The research I reference at the beginning of "Appendix" comes from "Comparative Anatomy and Phylogenic Distribution of the Mammalian Cecal Appendix" by H. F. Smith et al., which appeared in the *Journal of Evolutionary Biology*; "What Is the Function of the Human Appendix" by Loren G. Martin, which was published in *Scientific American*; and A. Zahid's published research in "The Vermiform Appendix: Not a Useless Organ," from the *Journal of the College of Physicians and Surgeons Pakistan*.

p. 65 / *The infant raises a shortened arm, and its mouth opens* refers to findings in "Hand-Mouth Coordination, Congenital Absence of Limb, and Evidence for Innate Body Schemas" by S. Gallagher et al. in *Brain and Cognition*.

p. 65 / In "Appendix," the phrase *nothing more than a means of being in another* and the three italicized phrases that follow come from *I, Afterlife: Essay in Mourning Time* by Kristen Prevallet.

pp. 67–68 / Much of the information found in the paragraph of "Joints" that begins "Most joints allow movement . . ." is a close paraphrase of information from *Emergency Care and Transportation of the Sick and Injured*, an American Academy of Orthopaedic Surgeons (AAOS) manual for EMTs. The last two sentences of the paragraph directly quote the AAOS text.

p. 68 / Carson's quote about famine comes from her short piece "Answer Scars," which appeared in *Wonderwater*.

p. 69 / In *The Dehumanization of Art and Other Writings on Art and Culture*, Ortega y Gasset writes, "Life is as far as possible from a subjective phenomenon. It is the most objective of all realities. It is a man's *I* finding itself submerged in precisely what is not himself, in the pure *other* which is his environment. To live is to be outside oneself, to realize oneself. . . . This unity of dramatic dynamism between the two elements, the I and the world—is life."

p. 70 / The mention of Osiris is a paraphrase of Ortega y Gasset's recounting of the Egyptian tale in *What Is Philosophy?*

p. 71 / *The one thing that keeps us out of connection* . . . and the stand-alone italicized lines that follow, as well as the research mentioned, comes from a June 2010 TEDx Houston lecture, "The Power of Vulnerability," by Brené Brown, research professor at University of Houston.

p. 72 / *Errors of form, the pattern of a life* is a line from Rickel's *Remanence*.

p. 73 / The NPR *All Things Considered* story referenced is "The Crossdressing Family Man Down the Block" by Eric Winick with Jay Allison and Larry Massett. It originally aired on November 8, 2008.

p. 73 / "Some researchers have speculated that we go through a sequence of love styles in our lives . . ." comes from a 1992 study by S. Hendrick and C. Hendrick, as quoted in Bianca P. Acevedo and Arthur Aron's 2011 article "Neural Correlates of Long-term Intense Romantic Love" in *Social, Cognitive, and Affective Neuroscience*. Additional information cited in this section regarding research at Stony Brook University comes from Acevedo and Aron's own findings.

p. 76 / *We are not born. We are not annihilated. So where are we? Shards of glass on the edge of breaking. On the verge of refracting a way through, to another world* comes from Prevallet's *I, Afterlife: Essay in Mourning Time.*

p. 79 / In his essay "Of the Nature and Origin of the Mind," Benedict de Spinoza writes: "*Reality and perfection* I use as synonymous terms." I have, obviously, played on his phrase. The structure for the "definitions" pages in this book is also adopted from his essay, which appears in the 1970 book *The Philosophy of the Body: Rejections of Cartesian Dualism.*

p. 81 / The Fanny Howe quotes come from *Indivisible.* She writes: *I would like to tell him that God has already crushed me into powder. Holy-talk has begun to calcify and bone into that powder too. Those refugees on the road, whose children, wives and husbands and friends were executed, know what it is to be left languishing in time. You can be buried alive in blue air and still walk around in a soft coat of gold.*

p. 82 / In *Plainwater*, Carson writes: *Like Socrates he fails to understand why travel should be such a challenge to the muscles of the heart, for other people.*

p. 83 / According to Carson in "Answer Scars," Flannery O'Connor noted in a 1957 Notre Dame speech, "to recognize the grotesque, you have to have some idea of what is not grotesque." Carson's reply, "The grotesque may take many forms."

p. 83 / "No one outruns this disease, no one survives it" is from a CBS Evening News segment titled "Early Onset Alzheimer's on the Rise." It aired on March 8, 2008.

p. 84 / *The city is nothing but a restless scaffolding* is a line from Boully's *The Book of Beginnings and Endings.*

p. 85 / In "Arteries," the lines "Oh, I told that one already . . . " and "I know my children, my grandchildren . . ." are from a January 12, 2009 StoryCorps interview with Mike and Judy Meagher that aired on Arizona Public Media on July 4, 2009.

p. 88 / "Lovely enough to *die into*" is from Boully's *The Book of Beginnings and Endings.*

p. 89 / In his 1646 book *On the Passions of the Soul,* Descartes writes: *The soul is of such a nature that it has no relation to extension, nor to the dimensions or other properties of matter composing the body, but only to the whole assemblage of its organs. . . . It does not become smaller on the removal of a part of the body. When, however, the assemblage of the bodily organs disintegrates, it itself, in its entirety, withdraws from the body.*

WORKS CITED

Acevedo, Bianca P., et al. "Neural Correlates of Long-term Intense Romantic Love." *Social, Cognitive, and Affective Neuroscience* 7.2 (2012): 145–59.

Allam, J. Shirine and Andrew H. Limper. "Idiopathic Pulmonary Fibrosis: Is It a Familial Disease?" *Current Opinion in Pulmonary Medicine* 12 (2006): 312–17.

Angiers, Natalie. "Bone: A Masterpiece of Elastic Strength." *The New York Times*, April 27, 2009. http://www.nytimes .com/2009/04/28/science/28angi.html.

Boully, Jenny. *The Book of Beginnings and Endings* (Louisville: Sarabande Books, 2007).

Brown, Brené. "The Power of Vulnerability." *TEDxHouston* lecture. Filmed June 2010. http://www.ted.com/talks/brene_brown_on_ vulnerability.html.

Carson, Anne. "Answer Scars." Vol. 2 of 4 books, slipcased together as *Wonderwater (Alice Offshore)*, by Roni Horn (Göttingen: Steidl, 2004).

Carson, Anne. *Plainwater: Essays and Poetry* (New York: Vintage Books, 2000).

Dillard, Annie. *For the Time Being* (New York: Vintage Books, 2000).

"Early Onset Alzheimer's on the Rise," from *CBS Evening News*. Aired March 8, 2008. www.cbsnews.com/stories/2008/03/08/ eveningnews/main3919747.shtml.

Engel, Jürgen and Hans Peter Bächinger. "Collagen: Structure, Stability and Folding of the Collagen Triple Helix." *Topics in Current Chemistry* 245 (2005): 7–33.

"Eyewitness Stories: Australia Fires." *BBC News*, Aired February 9, 2009. http://news.bbc.co.uk/2/hi/asia-pacific/7878191.stm.

Gallagher, S. et al. "Hand–Mouth Coordination, Congenital Absence of Limb, and Evidence for Innate Body Schemas." *Brain and Cognition* 38 (1998): 53–65.

Howe, Fanny. *Indivisible* (Los Angeles: Semiotext(e), 2000).

Irwin, Richard S. and James M. Rippe. *Manual of Intensive Care Medicine* (Philadelphia: Lippincott Williams and Wilkins, 2006).

Kauffman, Jeffrey, ed. *Awareness of Mortality* (Amityville: Baywood Publishing Company, 1995).

Kerley, Paul. "Slideshow: Fleeing the Flames." *BBC News*, Aired February 10, 2009. http://news.bbc.co.uk/2/hi/7879911.stm.

Kirchhoff, Palzkill, et al. "Preparing Families of Intensive Care Patients for Withdrawal of Life Support." *American Journal of Critical Care* 17 (2008): 113–21.

Martin, Loren. "What Is the Function of the Human Appendix?" *Scientific American*, October 21, 1999.

Mason, David P., et al. "Lung Transplantation for Idiopathic Pulmonary Fibrosis." *The Annals of Thoracic Surgery* 84 (2007): 1121–28.

MEDES: The Institute for Space Medicine and Physiology. http://www.medes.fr/home_en.html.

Murphy, Zoe. "Bushfire Dilemma: Flee or Fight." *BBC News*, Aired February 9, 2009. http://news.bbc.co.uk/2/hi/asia-pacific/7879132.stm.

Ortega y Gasset, Jose. *The Dehumanization of Art and Other Writings on Art and Culture* (Garden City: Doubleday, 1956).

Ortega y Gasset, Jose. *What Is Philosophy?* (New York: W. W. Norton, 1964).

Otu, Hasan H., Kamila Naxerova, Karen Ho, Handan Can, Nicole Nesbitt, Towia A. Libermann, and Seth J. Karp. "Restoration of Liver Mass after Injury Requires Proliferative and Not Embryonic Transcriptional Patterns." *The Journal of Biological Chemistry* 282 (2007): 11197–11204.

Pollack, Andrew, ed. *Emergency Care and Transportation of the Sick and Injured* (London: Jones and Bartlett Publishers, 2005).

Prevallet, Kristen. *I, Afterlife: Essay in Mourning Time* (Ithaca: Essay Press, 2011).

Rhoades, Rodney and David R. Bell, ed. *Medical Physiology: Principles for Clinical Medicine* (Baltimore: Lippincott, Williams, and Wilkins, 2008).

Rickel, Boyer. *Remanence* (Anderson: Parlor Press, 2008).

"Shark Therapy for Bizarre Bone Disease." *BBC News*. Aired March 24, 1999. http://news.bbc.co.uk/2/hi/health/302528.stm.

Skandalakis, L. J., L. E. Skandalakis, and P. N Skandalakis. *Surgical*

Anatomy and Technique (New York: Springer-Verlag, 2002).

Slovic, Paul. *"Perception* of Risk." *Science* 236 (1987): 280–85.

Smith, H. F., R. E. Fisher, M. L. Everett, A. D. Thomas, R. Bollinger, and W. Parker. "Comparative Anatomy and Phylogenic Distribution of the Mammalian Cecal Appendix." *Journal of Evolutionary Biology* 22 (2009): 1984–99.

Spicker, Stuart F., ed. *The Philosophy of the Body: Rejections of Cartesian Dualism* (Chicago: Quadrangle Books, 1970).

StoryCorps interview with Mike and Judy Meagher, Green Valley, Arizona. Jan 12, 2009. Aired on *Arizona Public Media,* July 4, 2009.

Tallis, Dr. Frank. *Love Sick: Love as a Mental Illness* (New York: Thunder's Mouth Press, 2005).

Thies, Kathleen, and John Travers. *Human Growth and Development through the Lifespan* (Thorofare: Jones & Bartlett Publishers, SLACK Incorporated, 2001).

Weil, Simone. *Gravity and Grace* (New York: GP Putnam's Sons, 1952).

Williams, Terry Tempest. *An Unspoken Hunger* (New York: Pantheon Books, 1994).

Winick, Eric, with Jay Allison and Larry Massett. "The Crossdressing Family Man down the Block." *NPR: All Things Considered.* Aired November 28, 2008.

Zahid, A. "The Vermiform Appendix: Not a Useless Organ." *Journal of College Physicians and Surgeons Pakistan* 4 (2004): 256–68.

SIGHTLINE BOOKS

The Iowa Series in Literary Nonfiction